Leader's Guide

The Devil Wants Me Fat
Get Your Mind Right and Your Body Tight

Stephanie R. Singleton

LEADER'S GUIDE

Original Copyright © 2015
Revised in 2016
PAUSE-66 Publishing

Disclaimer
This curriculum is not intended to provide medical advice or take the place of medical advice and treatment from your personal physician. The author does not take any responsibility for any possible consequences from any action taken by anyone reading or following the information in this book. If readers are taking prescription medications, they should consult with their physician and not take themselves off prescribed medicines without the proper supervision of a physician. Always consult your physician or other qualified health care professionals before undertaking any change in your physical regimen whether fasting, dieting, taking medications, or exercising.

ISBN-13: 978-0692669181
ISBN-10: 0692669183

TABLE OF CONTENTS

LEADER'S GUIDE

Thank you for choosing to start a *Pause on Fitness* group. This guide is designed to help facilitate discussion in your group setting. It includes an opening ice-breaker activity and some additional discussion questions. As the facilitator, you should also complete the assignments in your personal workbook and then use the leader's guide as an additional resource. Before your first meeting, participants should complete the first weekly assignment.

Facilitator Guidelines

- **Register your group -** If you would like your group to be open to members in your community and to receive updates, please complete the registration process for the *Pause on Fitness Groups* on;
www.pause66.com
- **Set a schedule for meeting dates** – After you have established a group, set up a day, time and location that work best. The discussions can take place in a variety of context: In person, conference calls, video chats or by other media outlets.
- **Be prepared** – As a leader, you are the example for your group to follow in completion of the assignments. Do not take

personally if the participants have not completed all of the questions. Encourage them to participate in the discussion and pray that they will have the time to complete the following week's assignment.

- **Respect the allotted time** – Both your time, as well as the other participants' time, is very valuable. Therefore, try to start and end on time. Each meeting should last between one-and-half to two hours, depending on the depth of the discussion. Encourage other members to be respectful of time limitations, so that everyone will have an opportunity to share. If your discussion leads to other pertinent issues within the group, consider continuing the conversation the following week if members agree.

- **Pray**- Commit to praying for your group members. Participants should be paired with another member to pray for them during the upcoming weeks. This will help members to connect with each other and reminding them to pray for someone else while God is working on their circumstances.

- **Facilitate and don't take over**- Remember, you are a participant in this group as well. Don't feel the need to answer all of the questions if you are not comfortable in sharing. Allow each member to share within his/her comfort zone.

Suggested Group Guidelines

It is important to share these guidelines with group members.

- **Group Facilitator** – This role should be assumed by a participant or someone who has previously completed the curriculum. This role can be rotated or continuous throughout the group meetings.
- **Accountability/Prayer Partner** – A trusted confidant who is willing to either meet with you on a weekly basis to share responses and pray for you during this program or someone who is a participant in the Pause on Fitness group.
- **Maintain Confidentiality** – A safe environment should be created in order to make participants feel comfortable sharing their personal experiences. Honor other members by not discussing their private information outside of the group.
- **Be Prepared** – Bring your bible and your *completed* assignments to each meeting.
- **Respect** – Please be mindful that some members may not feel comfortable sharing. It is also alright to have silence between the responses in the group to allow for reflection. When you do share your responses, please be attentive of any time limitations, so that others will have an opportunity to share as well.

How to Structure the Class

1. **Refreshments** – When you meet, consider having participants bring healthy refreshments to the meeting. The goal is to introduce members to healthy food options. If the refreshment requires preparation, volunteers should provide the recipe. Create a weekly sign-up sheet and confirm with the volunteer each week.

2. **Pray** – Open in prayer the first week. After the first week, ask another member if they would like to volunteer.

3. **Ice-Breaker Activity** – The activity should start each session and should last no longer than ten to fifteen minutes. Some of the activities are games, so you can provide prizes if you so desire.

4. **Testimony** – Give participants an opportunity to share their weekly fitness accomplishments.

5. **Motivational Memory Verse** – Ask for volunteers to recite it from memory.

6. **Weekly Overview** – Ask for a volunteer to read it aloud. Find out which members had an opportunity to complete the weekly assignments.

7. **Weight Management Challenge** – Ask for a volunteer to read it aloud and provide time for members to share.

8. **Exercise Prompts** - Ask for a volunteer to read it aloud and provide time for members to share.

9. **Group Discussion** – This is the most important part of the weekly meetings. Allow volunteers to share their responses. Some additional questions are added where needed to help facilitate discussion. It is alright for members to pass if they do not feel comfortable and it is alright to have times of silence for people to process their thoughts. Remember to always check the time because you may or may not get to cover all of the days in your allotted time.

10. **The Journey Ahead** - If time permits, participants can complete and share during the meeting.

11. **Pray** – End each meeting with prayer.

1
WHO HOLDS THE POWER?

- **Open in Prayer**
- **Ice Breaker Activity** – Have participants choose one M&M or Skittle candy at random. Each color should be assigned a question for participants to answer. The questions should be given only **after** participants have chosen a candy color. This activity gives members an opportunity to find commonalities and get to know each other.
  1) When you have 30 minutes of free time, how do you pass the time?
  2) If you could throw any kind of party, what would it celebrate and what would it be like?
  3) What chore do you absolutely hate doing?
  4) If you could learn to do anything, what would it be?
  5) What is your favorite song that "moves you"?
  6) If you could choose anyone, who would you pick as your mentor?
  7) What would be considered the perfect day for you?
- **Testimony**
- **Motivational Memory Verse** – The temptati-

ons in your life are no different from what others experience. And God is faithful. He will not allow the temptation to be more than you can stand. When you are tempted, he will show you a way out so that you can endure. **I Corinthians 10:13**

- **Weekly Overview** – Read aloud
- **Weight Management Challenge**
    1) Who has an updated physical exam or one scheduled?
- **Exercise Prompt**
    1) What exercise plan did you follow this week?
    2) *If participants did not engage in an activity, encourage them to try again the following week.*
- **Weekly Reading** – Chapters one and two

DAY ONE

Questions #1- #3 and #7 were individual assignments that do not need to be discussed.

- How many people completed their weekly meal planner?
- Did you discover anything about your eating habits?
- What is your plan to stay on track this week?

4. What stands out in the reading that you can apply to your own life?
Individual responses will vary.

5. Why are you starting this plan?
Individual responses will vary.

6. Do you feel like the devil wants you fat?
Individual responses will vary. Some participants may not be sure and others will relate obesity to gluttony. Participants should not feel the need to give a definitive answer because it will be discussed in more detail at a later time.

DAY TWO

Questions #8, #9 and #12 were individual assignments that do not need to be discussed.

10. You will also declare a thing, and it will be established for you; so light will shine on your ways. *Job 22:28*
Individual responses will vary.

What does this Scripture mean to you?

Form a plan or purpose something in your heart through your faith in God. Christians should not be disappointed if they do not see immediate results because they can trust that if God says anything in His word, He is faithful to fulfill it.

11. After personalizing Job 22:28, write down something that you decree before God to do in your own life. Think about every area of your life where you want to be fruitful and prosperous (health, career, marriage, spiritual life…).

Individual responses will vary.

DAY THREE

Questions #13, #14 and #16 were individual assignments that do not need to be discussed.

15. Create a personal prayer focused on your decree for your *life*.

Individual responses will vary. Have a volunteer read the sample decree. The decree should focus on what believers are trusting God to do. It should be positive and a declaration of faith.

Optional Discussion Question

a) Have you been praying your decree this week? If not, what has prevented you?

b) What plan can you create to incorporate your decree into your daily routine?

DAY FOUR

Questions #17- #18 were individual assignments that do not need to be discussed.

19. Review your meal planner for the first several days. What foods have been consistent in your daily consumption?
Individual responses will vary.

20. Do some research on the foods that you are consistently eating? Are your favorite foods considered nutritional?
Individual responses will vary. Ask participants to share the results of their research.

21. Now that you have been tracking what you have been eating for several days, review the foods on your list in question #19. Choose some new foods that replace at least five, if not more, with a healthier option on the chart provided for you on Table A.
Participants can share the items from their chart.

Optional Discussion Questions
a) Was it easy or difficult to find a food swap item for your chart?
b) Where did you research to find alternative food choices?

DAY FIVE

Questions #22, #23 and #25 were individual assignments that do not need to be discussed.

24. Review your food swap items and start to create some new healthier daily meal options on your meal planner.

Ask for volunteers to share some foods that will be included on their new meal planner.

Optional Discussion Question
a) What are your thoughts on the quote," If you fail to plan, you might as well plan to fail" in regards to your weight loss journey?

Reflections for the Journey Ahead
- If time permits, read over the questions and allow participants time to share responses or quiet time to complete it.
- Remind students to start to pre-plan their meals for the upcoming week.
- Assign or have participants choose an Accountability/Prayer Partner
- End in prayer

2

REFLECTION: BRIDGING THE PAST AND THE PRESENT

- **Open in Prayer**
- **Ice-Breaker Activity** – Give participants one minute to write down as many diet plans as they can think of before the time expires. Afterwards, ask the following questions:
  1) Which plans have you personally tried?
  2) Americans spend over 40 billion dollars a year on weight loss programs and products. Why do you think this is the case?

  Scripture Support:
  a. I praise you because I am fearfully and wonderfully made; your works are wonderful, I know that full well. **Psalms 139:14 Testimony**
- **Motivational Memory Verse** – For I know the plans I have for you," declares the LORD, "plans to prosper you and not to harm you, plans to give you hope and a future. **Jeremiah 29:11**
- **Weekly Overview**- Read aloud
- **Weight Management Challenge**
  1) What did you discover about the nutrition on the food labels in your

15

kitchen cabinets?

- **Exercise Prompt**
    1) What exercise plan did you follow this week? *If participants did not engage in an activity, encourage them to try again the following week.*
- **Weekly Reading** – Chapter three

DAY ONE

Questions #1- #3 were individual assignments that do not need to be discussed.

- How many people pre-planned their meals for the week?
- What unhealthy foods did you eat last week that were not listed on your planner?
- What is your plan to stay on track this week?

4. What stands out in the reading that you can apply to your own life?
Individual responses will vary.

5. Can you relate to any of the childhood experiences?
Individual responses will vary. The author discusses childhood experiences from her elementary, high school and college years.

6. What are your earliest recollections of your cycle of overeating (i.e. being teased as a child, a divorce, a failure, a pregnancy, stress on a job…)?
Individual responses will vary.

7. What feelings do you connect with those memories? When I reminisce, I felt lonely, self-pitying and disappointed, among others.
Individual responses will vary.

DAY TWO

Questions #8 - #9 were individual assignments that do not need to be discussed.

10. What are your physical fitness goals?
Individual responses will vary.

Optional Discussion Questions
a) Have any of you ever reached a fitness goal? If so, how long did you maintain your success?

11. What is a realistic time frame for achieving this goal?
Individual responses will vary.

Optional Discussion Questions
a) Who was able to cut their calories this week?
b) What did you sacrifice in order to cut those calories?

DAY THREE

Questions #12 - #13 were individual assignments that do not need to be discussed.

14. Think of four to six words or labels that were used to describe you in your youth and early adult stages. Two personal labels that I discussed in chapter three were "chubby" and "smart girl." After each label do the following: (1) Decide whether or not that label was positive or negative for you (2) Indicate who gave you that label (3)

Explain how or why you were given that label.
Individual responses will vary.

15. Choose one of the labels that made the most impact on you. Write about either a *positive* or *negative* memory associated with that label.
Individual responses will vary.

DAY FOUR
Questions #16 - #17 were individual assignments that do not need to be discussed.

18. As you review the negative words and labels from day three that were spoken into your life, which of the labels do you still identify with today? How have they impacted you?
Individual responses will vary.

Optional Discussion Question
a) How did you feel reflecting on the labels that were assigned to you?

DAY FIVE
Questions #19 - #20 were individual assignments that do not need to be discussed.

21. These assignments may have challenged you to recognize that there are people in your life that you need to distance yourself from in order to break free of whatever is holding you back. Are there people in your life that fit into these

categories?
Individual responses will vary.

22. Scripture Reference: Don't team up with those who are unbelievers. How can righteousness be a partner with wickedness? How can light live with darkness? *2 Corinthians 6:14 (NLT)*

23. Who are the people from which you need to distance yourself?
Individual responses will vary.

<u>Optional Discussion Question</u>
a) If the people that assigned the negative labels to you are still a part of your life, how important is it for you to share your feelings with them?

24. Will separating yourself help you?
Individual responses will vary.

25. Scripture Reference: And now, dear brothers and sisters, one final thing. Fix your thoughts on what is true, and honorable, and right, and pure, and lovely, and admirable. Think about things that are excellent and worthy of praise. *Philippians 4:8 (NLT)*

26. Pray this prayer together:

Dear Jesus,

I forgive everyone in my life that has ever spoken a word curse or said a negative comment to me. I will not harbor any negative thoughts towards them and will not allow those thoughts to penetrate my mind or my heart ever again. Since you have given me power over Satan and his attacks, I ask you to close any doorway that has been opened by Satan into my life. I give you back the keys and allow you to have control in this area. I believe what I John 5:18 says about me. I am your child and the evil one cannot touch me because I am secure in you.

Amen

Reflections for the Journey Ahead
- If time permits, read over the questions and allow participants time to answer complete the assignment and share responses. Otherwise, they may complete it on their own time.
- Remind students to pre-plan their meals for the upcoming week.
- End in prayer and remind participants to stay in contact with their partners throughout the week.

3

You Are an Overcomer!

- **Open in Prayer**
- **Ice-Breaker Activity-** Select a volunteer before the start of the class to mingle with the rest of the group. After some time has passed, ask the volunteer to leave the room and give each group member paper and pencil. Tell them to describe in as much detail as possible what the volunteer was wearing in sixty seconds.

1) Do you ever feel scrutinized, like you are on display? When does this occur?
2) Do you ever feel like no one notices you? Why do you have those feelings?

Scripture Support:

   a. And the very hairs on your head are all numbered. **Matthew 10:30**

   b. The LORD will work out his plans for my life—for your faithful love, O LORD, endures forever. Don't abandon me, for you made me. **Psalms 138:8**

   c. Be strong and courageous. Do not be afraid or terrified because of them, for the LORD your God goes with you; he will never leave you nor forsake you. **Deuteronomy 31:6**

God wants His children to always walk in confidence knowing that He is walking beside them every step of this journey.

- **Testimony**
- **Motivational Memory Verse –** But the Holy Spirit produces this kind of fruit in our lives: love, joy, peace, patience, kindness, goodness, faithfulness, gentleness, and self-control. There is no law against these things! **Galatians 5:22-23**
- **Weekly Overview-** Read aloud
- **Weight Management Challenge –** What foods did you eliminate this week?
- **Exercise Prompt**
  1) What exercise plan did you follow this week?
     If participants did not engage in an activity, encourage them to try again the following week.
- **Weekly Reading** – Chapters four and five

DAY ONE

Questions #1- #3 were individual assignments that do not need to be discussed.

- How many people pre-planned their meals for the week?
- What unhealthy foods did you eat last week that were not listed on your planner?
- What is your plan to stay on track this week?

4. What stands out in the reading that you can apply to your own life?
Individual responses will vary.

DAY TWO

Questions #5- #6 were individual assignments that do not need to be discussed.

7. Listed below are obstacles that many have faced at one time or another in their lifetime. What does God say to you personally through each verse?
Individual responses will vary.

- *Fear* - **Deuteronomy 31:6** So be strong and courageous! Do not be afraid and do not panic before them. For the LORD your God will personally go ahead of you. He will neither fail you nor abandon you.
  Sample: Stephanie, you do not have to ever fear when you share the life lessons that I taught you with others. I have already

paved the way and given you territory to claim for My kingdom.

- *Anxiety* - **Philippians 4:6** Be anxious for nothing, but in everything by prayer and supplication, with thanksgiving, let your requests be made known to God.
We are not to worry about anything, but we should let God know what we need.
- *Feeling unloved* - **I John 3:1** Behold what manner of love the Father has bestowed on us, that we should be called children of God!* Therefore the world does not know us,* because it did not know Him.
God loves us so much that he calls us His children.
- *Abandonment* - **Psalms 27:10** When my father and my mother forsake me, Then the LORD will take care of me.
I never have to worry about anything.
- *Loneliness* - **John 14:16** And I will ask the Father, and he will give you another advocate to be with you forever.
The Lord will never leave me alone.
- *Rejection* - **Proverbs 18:24** A man of many companions may come to ruin, but there is a friend who sticks closer than a brother.
Jesus will always be my friend even when others may turn their back on me.
- *Discontentment* - **Philippians 4:11** I am not saying this because I am in need, for I have learned to be content whatever the

circumstances.

Even when things don't happen the way that I desire, I need to learn how to still have joy.

- *Unforgiveness* - **Matthew 6:15** But if you do not forgive men their sins, your Father will not forgive your sins.

  In order for me to be forgiven by God, I cannot hold on to hurts and offenses. I have to release it to God.

- *Lack of trust for provision* - **Matthew 6:26** Look at the birds of the air; they do not sow or reap or store away in barns, and yet your heavenly Father feeds them. Are you not much more valuable than they?

  My Heavenly Father sees me as the most valuable creation on this world, therefore He will always provide for me.

DAY THREE

Questions #8- #9 were individual assignments that do not need to be discussed.

10. There are many other scriptures that relate to these issues. The word of God instructs us in 2 Timothy 2:15 to study the word of God so that we can be guided in truth. Find more scriptures that relate to these areas.

Additional Scriptural References

- Fear : 2 Timothy 1:7, Psalms 34:7, Matthew 10:31
- Anxiety: Matthew 6:34, Isaiah 40:31, Psalms 55:22
- Feeling Unloved: Psalms 139:1-3, Genesis 1:27, I John 3:1
- Abandonment: Romans 8:28, 2 Corinthians 4:9, Psalms 34:18
- Loneliness: Matthew 28:20, I Samuel 12:22, Isaiah 41:10
- Rejection: John 14:18, Psalms 147:3, Deuteronomy 4:31
- Discontentment: Hebrews 13:5, Psalms 37:4, Matthew 6:33
- Unforgiveness: Luke 23:43, I Corinthians 13:4-7, Ephesians 4:31-32
- Lack of trust for provision: Philippians 4:19, John 15:7, Matthew 21:22

DAY FOUR
Questions #11- #12 were individual assignments that do not need to be discussed.

13. **Review the list of emotions and issues from Day Two. Identify the ones that you struggle with the most.**
Individual responses will vary.

Optional Discussion Question
a) How was the reflection process?

14. How long have you dealt with these feelings?
Individual responses will vary.

15. Why do you think these issues are still stumbling blocks for you?
Individual responses will vary.

16. Which one of these issues do you have the strongest emotional memory attached to it?
Individual responses will vary.

17. It is normal to experience these emotions, but it is important to never allow them to take root in your life again.

Dear Jesus,

I ask you to forgive me for holding on to things in my life in which I know you want to provide healing. Please help me to continue to identify any issues that have caused me to not be in complete fellowship with you. I want to recognize everything that is holding me back from my wholeness. Please search my heart God and know all of my anxious thoughts. Whatever evil ways that I have within me, I ask you to bring them into the light, so that I will be healed.

Amen.

DAY FIVE
Questions #18- #19 were individual assignments that do not need to be discussed.

20. What other areas has God revealed that are current challenges in your life? Identify those areas and find a scripture that will challenge you not to ignore it, so that it continues to be a spiritual hindrance for you. Psalms 139:23 says, "Search me God, and know my heart; test me and know my anxious thoughts."

Optional Discussion Questions
a) What other areas did God reveal to you?
b) How do you feel about the revelation?

21. Reflect on the times that you ate items that were not on your daily meal planner and the times when you failed to exercise. What feelings did you experience?
Individual responses will vary.

22. Have you noticed any connections between your eating patterns and the emotions discussed in day four?
Individual responses will vary.

23. What attributes are associated with God in the following scriptures?
Individual responses will vary.

- **Isaiah 41:10** – So do not fear, for I am with you; do not be dismayed, for I am your God. I will strengthen you and help you; I will uphold you with my righteous right hand.

(He will always be with you; Righteousness; Give you strength)

- **Romans 5:8**- But God demonstrates his own love for us in this: While we were still sinners, Christ died for us. (A loving God; A God who sacrificed His life for you)
- **I John 4:16**- And so we know and rely on the love God has for us. God is love. Whoever lives in love lives in God, and God in them. (A loving God)
- **Romans 8:31**- What, then, shall we say in response to these things? If God is for us, who can be against us? (God will support you when you are following His ways)
- **2 Chronicles 20:15**- He said: "Listen, King Jehoshaphat and all who live in Judah and Jerusalem! This is what the LORD says to you: 'Do not be afraid or discouraged because of this vast army.' For the battle is not yours, but God's."(God will fight for you)

24. Based on what we know about our Father in heaven, should we ever condemn ourselves or give up hope during this journey when mistakes are made?

No one should continue to condemn themself because of failures because the hope and faith of healing comes with a relationship with Jesus Christ.

25. If we do, who has won according to John 10:10?
Scripture Reference: The thief's purpose is to steal and kill and destroy. My purpose is to give them a rich and satisfying life. John 10:10
The thief is the devil.

Reflections for the Journey Ahead
- If time permits, read over the questions and allow participants time to answer complete the assignment and share responses. Otherwise, they may complete it on their own time.
- Remind students to pre-plan their meals for the upcoming week
- End in prayer and remind participants to stay in contact with their partners throughout the week.

4

IT'S TIME TO
BREAK THE CHAINS

- **Open in Prayer**
- **Ice-Breaker Activity-** Place three or four household objects into a soft bag or a tied handkerchief (watch, pencil, glasses, candle, spoon, paperclip...). Pass the bag around the room and give participants 5 seconds to feel the contents. After everyone has had a turn, participants should try to identify the objects.
  1) What was the most challenging part of the activity?
  2) Have you ever felt like people make judgments about you without taking enough time to get to know who you really are on the inside? How does that make you feel?

Scripture Support:
  a. But the LORD said to Samuel, "Do not consider his appearance or his height, for I have rejected him. The LORD does not look at the things people look at. People look at the outward appearance, but the LORD looks at the heart." **I Samuel 16:7**

- **Testimony**
- **Motivational Memory Verse**

  Now all glory to God, who is able, through his mighty power at work within us, to accomplish infinitely more than we might ask or think. **Ephesians 3:20**
- **Weekly Overview**- Read aloud
- **Weight Management Challenge**
  1) What health magazines are you reading?
  2) What foods did you identify that you need to avoid?
- **Exercise Prompt**
  1) Did anyone switch to a morning exercise routine?
  2) What exercise plan did you follow this week?

     If participants did not engage in an activity, encourage them to try again the following week.
- **Weekly Reading –** Chapter six

DAY ONE

Questions #1- #3 were individual assignments that do not need to be discussed.

- How many people pre-planned their meals for the week?
- What unhealthy foods did you eat last week that were not listed on your planner?
- What is your plan to stay on track this week?

4. What stands out in the reading that you can apply to your own life?

Individual responses will vary.

DAY TWO

Questions #5- #6 were individual assignments that do not need to be discussed.

7. As you read in chapter six of the book, one of the shackles that I experienced was doubt that God is a healer. What are the restraints or limitations that you have placed on God?

Individual responses will vary.

8. What are the restraints or limitations that you have placed on yourself?

Individual responses will vary.

9. How do these restraints impact you in your personal faith and fitness journey?

Individual responses will vary.

10. Scriptural References:

a. *For we are God's handiwork, created in Christ Jesus to do good works, which God prepared in advance for us to do.* **Ephesians 2:10**

b. *Don't you realize that your body is the temple of the Holy Spirit, who lives in you and was given to you by God? You do not belong to yourself, [20] for God bought you with a high price. So you must honor God with your body. I Corinthians 6:19-20*

What personal connections can you make between *Recognizing* **and** *Receiving* **the Biblical truths in the verses above?**

Individual responses will vary.

As Christians we should be mindful and recognize that the Holy Spirit dwells within us once we submit to Christ. Whenever limits are placed on God, it hinders whatever He wants to do in a believer's life. Unless a believer is willing to submit his will and desires in order to receive whatever God wants to do, there will always be a blockage.

DAY THREE

Questions #11- #12 were individual assignments that do not need to be discussed.

13. The motivational memory verse for the week says: Now all glory to God, who is able, through his mighty power at work within us, to

accomplish infinitely more than we might ask or think (Ephesians 3:20). Be honest with yourself. Do you really believe and receive this Truth in your own life? If your answer is no, what happened to make you stop believing this Truth? *Individual responses will vary.*

14. If your answer is yes, do the decisions that you make and the conversations that you engage in line up with this Biblical Truth?
Individual responses will vary.

<u>Optional Discussion Question</u>
a) Do your words and actions reflect fear or faith? How do you know?

15. Give an example of how God has enabled you to accomplish something great in your own life.
Individual responses will vary.

16. Prayer

Dear Heavenly Father,

I ask you to forgive me for not allowing my thoughts to line up with the truth in Your words. I have allowed my self-imposed limitations to be a hindrance to me moving forward in my life. I now will line my ways to your ways and go forward in the truth that you have my best interest. I trust that You are writing my life story and You know every chapter, every sentence, every word and most importantly You know how it ends. You want me to be successful in this area of my life and I will yield my desires to Your desires.

Amen

DAY FOUR

Questions #17- #18 were individual assignments that do not need to be discussed.

19. What do these Scriptures say about faith?

- Now faith is confidence in what we hope for and assurance about what we do not see. **Hebrews 11:1**
- And without faith it is impossible to please God, because anyone who comes to him must believe that he exists and that he rewards those who earnestly seek him. **Hebrews 11:6**

20. In what areas of your life is your faith being tested the most?

Individual responses will vary.

21. On a scale of 1-5 (one is poor and five is good), how do you feel like you handle the test of faith before you?

Individual responses will vary.

Optional Discussion Question
a) Why did you give yourself this rating?

22. On a scale of 1-5 (one is seldom and five is often), how has eating food been a way to cope with the challenge?
Individual responses will vary.

<u>Optional Discussion Question</u>
a) Why did you give yourself that rating?

23. Write down the following scriptures:
- Trust in the LORD with all your heart; do not depend on your own understanding. **Proverbs 3:5**
- Give all your worries and cares to God, for he cares about you. **I Peter 5:7**

24. Pray about your responses in questions #21 and #22. What is God personally saying to you in these verses?
Individual responses will vary.

DAY FIVE
Questions #25- #26 were individual assignments that do not need to be discussed.

27. Do you recognize a connection between the areas in which you are being tested and your weight gain? If so, what is it?
Individual responses will vary.

28. What does James 1:3 say about faith?
- For you know that when your faith is tested,

your endurance has a chance to grow. **James 1:3**

29. How does your faith impact you on your journey towards weight loss?
Individual responses will vary.

30. What do you feel like God is trying to teach you in this battle?
Individual responses will vary.

Reflections for the Journey Ahead
- If time permits, read over the questions and allow participants time to answer complete the assignment and share responses. Otherwise, they may complete it on their own time.
- Remind students to pre-plan their meals for the upcoming week
- End in prayer and remind participants to stay in contact with their partners throughout the week.

5

YOU ARE WHO GOD SAYS THAT YOU ARE

- **Open in Prayer**
- **Ice Breaker Activity** – Two volunteers are needed. One will be blindfolded and the other one should be given a picture of an item such as a cake, a cup, a hanger, a t-shirt, a watch, a radio, a lamp, a comb or a brush, etc. The participant must instruct the blindfolded participant how to draw the item in a two minute time limit. The person who is blindfolded should not have any prior knowledge of the drawing. When time expires, compare the drawing to the picture.
  1) What was the most challenging part of the activity?
  2) Did you ever get frustrated?
  3) How challenging was it for you to try to figure out what to do without seeing anything in front of you?

Scripture Support:
  a. My child, listen to what I say, and treasure my commands. Tune your ears to wisdom, and concentrate on understanding. Cry out for insight, and ask for understanding. Search for

them as you would for silver; seek them like hidden treasures. Then you will understand what it means to fear the LORD, and you will gain knowledge of God. **Proverbs 2:1-5**

Sometimes you will not be able to see the whole picture of what God is doing in your life on your fitness journey. Just tune your ears to hear exactly what He wants you to do.

- **Testimony**
- **Motivational Memory Verse**
- Be on guard. Stand firm in the faith. Be courageous. Be strong. **I Corinthians 16:13**
- **Weekly Overview**- Read aloud
- **Weight Management Challenge**
  1) Who was able to eat less because they chewed their food more slowly?
- **Exercise Prompt**
  1) What exercise plan did you follow this week?
  If participants did not participate in an activity, encourage them to try again the following week.
- **Weekly Reading** – Chapters seven and eight

DAY ONE
Questions #1- #3 were individual assignments that do not need to be discussed.
- How many people pre-planned their meals for the week?
- What unhealthy foods did you eat last week that were not listed on your planner?
- What is your plan to stay on track this week?

4. What stands out in the reading that you can apply to your own life?
Individual responses will vary.

DAY TWO
Questions #5- #6 were individual assignments that do not need to be discussed.

7. We should treat our body as something to be treasured. Name at least one thing that you love about your body. (This does not have to be shared during group discussion)
Individual responses will vary.

8. When you think of your body, what thoughts or images come to your mind?
Individual responses will vary.

9. What does your body inhibit you from doing that you would want to do?
Individual responses will vary.

DAY THREE

Questions #10- #11 were individual assignments that do not need to be discussed.

12. How we present ourselves to others says a lot about our personality and self-confidence. What do you believe your body says to the world about who you are? For example: *I love myself, I am confident, I have low self-esteem, I am lazy...)*
Individual responses will vary.

Optional Discussion Question
a) Why do you believe that you give off that impression? (Ex: Style of dress, idiosyncrasies, hairstyle, faith, relationships...)

13. What do you want your body to say to others about who you are? Do the answers to questions #8 and #12 differ from the answer to this question?
Individual responses will vary.

14. What does your faith walk say to the people in your life and those that you encounter? Be as honest as possible. (This does not have to be shared during class discussion).
Individual responses will vary.

15. What do you want your faith walk to say to the people in your life and those that you encounter?
Individual responses will vary.

DAY FOUR

Questions #16- #17 were individual assignments that do not need to be discussed.

18. According to the following scriptures, who are you in Christ?
Individual responses will vary.

- *Romans 8:28* - And we know that in all things God works for the good of those who love him, who have been called according to his purpose. (I am called according to God's purpose for things to work for my good although it doesn't always appear that way).

- *2 Corinthians 1:21-22* - It is God who enables us, along with you, to stand firm for Christ. He has commissioned us, and he has identified us as his own by placing the Holy Spirit in our hearts as the first installment that guarantees everything he has promised us. (God qualifies me to do what He needs me to do. God's Spirit is His promise that His plans will come to pass).

- *Philippians 3:20* - But we are citizens of heaven, where the Lord Jesus Christ lives. And we are eagerly waiting for him to return as our Savior. (I am a citizen of heaven).

- *Colossians 3:2-3* - Think about the things of heaven, not the things of earth. For you died to this life, and your real life is hidden with Christ in God. (My life is following the plans of God).
- *I John 5:18* - We know that God's children do not make a practice of sinning, for God's Son holds them securely, and the evil one cannot touch them. (I can live a life following the commands of God; the devil cannot harm me as long as I am secure in my relationship with Christ).
- *John 15:16* - You didn't choose me. I chose you. I appointed you to go and produce lasting fruit, so that the Father will give you whatever you ask for, using my name.(I was chosen for God to fulfill a purpose. While I am fulfilling that purpose, my Heavenly Father will provide everything that I need).
- *2 Corinthians 6:1* - As God's co-workers we urge you not to receive God's grace in vain. (I should not take the grace that I have been given by God for granted).
- *Ephesians 2:6* - For he raised us from the dead along with Christ and seated us with him in the heavenly realms because we are united with Christ Jesus. (I am united with Christ).
- *Ephesians 3:12* - Because of Christ and our faith in him, we can now come boldly and confidently into God's presence. (I can come

to God without fear).

- *Philippians 4:13* - For I can do everything through Christ, who gives me strength. (Jesus enables me to do anything as long as He is the focus).

DAY FIVE

Questions #19- #20 were individual assignments that do not need to be discussed.

21. There are many other scriptures that relate to the authority of a believer in Christ Jesus. The Word of God says that all Scripture is inspired by God and is useful to teach us what is true and to make us realize what is wrong in our lives. It corrects us when we are wrong and teaches us to do what is right. God uses it to prepare and equip His people to do every good work **(2 Timothy 3:16-17). What other scriptures will remind you of God's truth in your life.**
Individual responses will vary.

22. Whose words always speak truth? God. Many of us have heard this famous adage in many different versions:

- **Watch your thoughts. They determine your words.**
- **Watch your words. They determine your thinking.**
- **Watch your thinking. They determine your habits.**

- Watch your habits. They determine your character.
- Watch your character. It will determine your destiny and ultimately your fulfillment of God's promises in your life.

23. Do you agree with this adage? What part of the adage challenges you the most and why?
Individual responses will vary.

Dear Jesus,

Search my heart heavenly Father. Guide me in all truth and righteousness. Show me where I have fallen short in letting my light shine in this world for others to see Your Glory. Forgive me for the times that I have not accepted who I am in You and not walked in the confidence and knowledge that You love me and have a great destiny in store for me. Lead me from this time forward in showing every person that I encounter the abundant life that You have freely given to me.

Amen

24. Does the image that you display to the world line up with a Biblical standard? What is God saying to you?
Individual responses will vary.

Reflections for the Journey Ahead

- If time permits, read over the questions and allow participants time to answer complete the assignment and share responses. Otherwise, they may complete it on their own time.
- Remind students to pre-plan their meals for the upcoming week
- End in prayer and remind participants to stay in contact with their partners throughout the week.

6
LEAN ON ME

- **Open in Prayer**
- **Ice Breaker Activity** – Choose one volunteer to be blindfolded and another volunteer to give instructions. The non-blindfolded participant will give directions to the blindfolded participant on how to walk from one side of the room to the other. The participant will have to try to avoid obstacles along the path while relying on the voice of the person giving her directions.
  1) What was the most challenging part of the activity?
  2) Did you ever get frustrated?
  3) How challenging is it for you to listen to the voice of God on your journey when you can't always see the path that is before you?

Scripture Support:
  a. This is my command—be strong and courageous! Do not be afraid or discouraged. For the LORD your God is with you wherever you go." **Joshua 1:9**

It can get frustrating at times when you encounter obstacles and you can't figure out what to do. Always trust that God will always lead you every step of the way.

- **Testimony**
- **Motivational Memory Verse**
  God is our refuge and strength, always ready
  to help in times of trouble.
  Psalms 46:1
- **Weekly Overview** – Read aloud.
- **Weight Management**
  1) Which challenge did you focus on this
  week?
- **Exercise Prompt**
  1) What exercise plan did you follow this
  week?
  *If participants did not engage in an activity,
  encourage them to try again the following
  week.*
- **Weekly Reading** – Chapter nine

DAY ONE

Questions #1- #3 were individual assignments that do not need to be discussed.

- How many people pre-planned their meals for the week?
- What unhealthy foods did you eat last week that were not listed on your planner?
- What is your plan to stay on track this week?

4. What stands out in the reading that you can apply to your own life?

Individual responses will vary.

DAY TWO

Questions #5- #6 were individual assignments that do not need to be discussed.

Refer to Lesson One, *You better Recognize.*

- Lest Satan should take advantage of us; for we are not ignorant of his devices. **2 Corinthians 2:11**

7. What devices has Satan used to trap you into a lifestyle of overeating?

Individual responses will vary (low self-esteem, guilt, boredom, feeling unloved, self-hatred...).

8. Now that you have identified the trap, what lessons have you learned so far to escape it?

Individual responses will vary.

Refer to Lesson Two, *Whip it into shape*
- But I discipline my body and bring *it* into subjection, lest, when I have preached to others, I myself should become disqualified. **1 Corinthians 9:27**
- Beloved, I pray that you may prosper in all things and be in health, just as your soul prospers. **3 John 1:2**
- As a door swings back and forth on its hinges, so the lazy person turns over in bed. **Proverbs 26:14**

9. (A) Have you been consistent with the weekly exercise prompts?
Individual responses will vary.
(B) What has motivated you to discipline yourself to exercise or why are you still having problems?
Individual responses will vary.

DAY THREE
Questions #10- #11 were individual assignments that do not need to be discussed.

Refer to Lesson Three, *Put a knife to my throat?*
- Therefore, since we are surrounded by such a great cloud of witnesses, let us throw off everything that hinders and the sin that so easily entangles. And let us run with perseverance the race marked out for us. **Hebrews 12:1**
- If you are a big eater, put a knife to your

throat. **Proverbs 23:2**

12. What issues have you identified that are slowing you down from reaching optimal health and fitness?
Individual responses will vary (Unforgiveness, self-hatred, jealousy, strife, gluttony…).

13. What overindulgences are you still tempted with most often?
Individual responses will vary.

14. What Scripture(s) can you use to help you through the temptation?
Individual responses will vary.

15. Refer to the lessons from these scriptures; what habits should you model in your lifestyle for non-believers to reflect Christ?
Individual responses will vary (doing good deeds, consulting God before making decisions, worshipping God, doing the work that Christ has called us to do…).

- In the same way, let your light shine before others, that they may see your good deeds and glorify your Father in heaven. **Matthew 5:16**
- In all your ways acknowledge Him, and He shall direct your paths. **Proverbs 3:6**
- But the hour is coming, and now is, when the true worshipers will worship the Father in

spirit and truth; for the Father is seeking such to worship Him. **John 4:23**

- God decided in advance to adopt us into his own family by bringing us to himself through Jesus Christ. This is what he wanted to do, and it gave him great pleasure. **Ephesians 1:5**
- For we are God's masterpiece. He has created us anew in Christ Jesus, so we can do the good things he planned for us long ago. **Ephesians 2:10**
- And I am certain that God, who began the good work within you, will continue his work until it is finally finished on the day when Christ Jesus returns. **Philippians 1:6**

DAY FOUR

Questions #16- #17 were individual assignments that do not need to be discussed.

Refer to Lesson Five, *Be thou Loosed!*

- He personally carried our sins in his body on the cross so that we can be dead to sin and live for what is right. By his wounds you are healed. 1 Peter 2:24
- But he was pierced for our rebellion, crushed for our sins. He was beaten so we could be whole. He was whipped so we could be healed. Isaiah 53:5
- The LORD passed in front of Moses, calling out, "Yahweh! The LORD! The God of

compassion and mercy! I am slow to anger and filled with unfailing love and faithfulness. **Exodus 34:6**

18. In what area(s) of your physical or emotional life do you trust in God to heal?
Individual responses will vary.

19. Define yourself in Christ Jesus.
Individual responses will vary. I am a woman who is loved, a daughter who is free to pursue the dreams that God has given me, and a warrior who will fight to maintain a high standard of integrity that reflects her Father in heaven. Who are you?

Optional Discussion Questions
a) How has placing your identity declarations around the house impacted you?

Refer to Lesson Six, *This is my house*
- Do you not know that you are the temple of God and that the Spirit of God dwells in you? **1 Corinthians 3:16**
- Then David danced before the LORD with all his might; and David was wearing a linen ephod. **2 Samuel 6:14**
- Let all that I am praise the LORD; with my whole heart, I will praise his holy name. Psalms 103:1

Next week you will have a day of fasting. Spend time

preparing your Spirit to focus on what you are asking God to heal in your life (refer to question #18). Consult your doctor regarding any health concerns and modify accordingly.

20. What are your feelings regarding fasting?
Individual responses will vary.

21. Prayer:

Dear Heavenly Father,

I thank you for the opportunity to dedicate time to spend in Your presence. I present the areas that You have revealed to me that need to be healed so that I can be whole again. You did not create me to be broken and fragmented, but to be complete in You. I give to You_____ (say the areas that you are asking God to heal). As I trust in You completely for my healing, I know that I can do all things through You because You make all things new.

Amen

DAY FIVE
Questions #22- #23 were individual assignments that do not need to be discussed.

Refer to Lesson Seven: *Is it a sin to be fat?*
- For what I am doing, I do not understand. For what I will to do, that I do not practice; but what I hate, that I do. If, then, I do what I will not to do, I agree with the law that it is

good. But now, it is no longer I who do it, but sin that dwells in me. **Romans 7:15-17**

- But the fruit of the Spirit is love, joy, peace, longsuffering, kindness, goodness, faithfulness, gentleness, self-control. Against such there is no law. **Galatians 5:22-23**

- For the flesh lusts against the Spirit, and the Spirit against the flesh; and these are contrary to one another, so that you do not do the things that you wish. **Galatians 5:17**

- For though we live in the world, we do not wage war as the world does. [4] The weapons we fight with are not the weapons of the world. On the contrary, they have divine power to demolish strongholds. [5] We demolish arguments and every pretension that sets itself up against the knowledge of God, and we take captive every thought to make it obedient to Christ. **2 Corinthians 10:3-5**

- So now there is no condemnation for those who belong to Christ Jesus. And because you belong to him, the power of the life-giving Spirit has freed you from the power of sin that leads to death. **Romans 8:1-2**

24. What was your answer to the question, "Do you think the devil wants you fat?" (Refer to week one)

Individual responses will vary.

25. Has your answer remained consistent throughout the readings? Share your thoughts.
Individual responses will vary.

26. "For many, of whom I have often told you and now tell you even with tears, walk as enemies of the cross of Christ. Their end is destruction, their god is their belly, and they glory in their shame, with minds set on earthly things." Philippians 3:18-19. Webster dictionary defines gluttony as the act or habit of eating or drinking too much. Do you sometimes feel challenged with whether or not your lifestyle follows the biblical guidelines of gluttony? Write your thoughts.
Individual responses will vary.

27. Review the Scripture in Philippians on gluttony. Did you notice that the Scripture and definition does not focus on a person's physical size or weight? What is considered too much for one person to eat may be different for a man or woman who has a different height or physique. The Scripture allows us to focus on our relationship with Christ as opposed to the calories we consume. The discipline of eating and the reasons why one overeats is where the attention should be focused. Write your thoughts on the line provided. During your prayer time, share them with God.
Individual responses will vary.

a) What are your thoughts on gluttony?
b) Have you ever considered this perspective?

Homework: Have students write a letter to themselves about what they want to accomplish in one year. This should not be limited to weight loss goals (graduation, new career, children, marriage, mended relationships, spiritual goals…). Students should bring their letters to the next meeting.

Reflections for the Journey Ahead
- If time permits, read over the questions and allow participants time to answer complete the assignment and share responses. Otherwise, they may complete it on their own time.
- Remind students to pre-plan their meals for the upcoming week.
- End in prayer and remind participants to stay in contact with their partners throughout the week.

7

CREATING A PLAN

- **Open in Prayer**
- **Ice Breaker Activity** – Students have the opportunity to share their one year goals with the members of the group. After sharing, pray over the letters and give each member an envelope to place the letter inside. Each participant should write on the envelope and not open until one year from the present date.
  1) How did you feel about this activity?
  2) Did you create realistic goals?
  3) What will be your biggest obstacle?

  Scripture Support:
  > a. Commit to the LORD whatever you do, and he will establish your plans.
  > **Proverbs 16:3**
- **Testimony**
- **Motivational Memory Verse**
  Don't copy the behavior and customs of this world, but let God transform you into a new person by changing the way you think. Then you will learn to know God's will for you, which is good and pleasing and perfect.
  Romans 12:2
- **Weekly Overview** – Read aloud
- **Weight Management Challenge**

1) Who changed their plate size?
2) Who followed the recommended serving size?
3) Were you satisfied after you ate?

- **Exercise Prompt**

1) What exercise plan did you follow this week?

If participants did not participate in an activity, encourage them to try again the following week.

- **Weekly Reading** – Chapter ten

DAY ONE

Questions #1- #3 were individual assignments that do not need to be discussed.

- How many people pre-planned their meals for the week?
- What unhealthy foods did you eat last week that were not listed on your planner?
- What is your plan to stay on track this week?

4. What stands out in the reading that you can apply to your own life?

Individual responses will vary.

DAY TWO

Questions #5- #6 were individual assignments that do not need to be discussed.

7. In chapter ten, I self-reflected on lessons that God taught me on my journey. I also posed four questions to help decide whether or not some of the practices that I learned from my family were beneficial to my spiritual life.

The author provided her personal responses to the questions in the workbook.

1) Identify the Habit/Behavior
2) Does it help me to grow in my spiritual life?
3) Does it build me up as a person?
4) Does it line up with biblical principles?
5) Does the habit/behavior cause negative consequences in your family tree?
6) Identify the lesson that was learned

8. Describe yourself as a person. Use as many adjectives as needed. (Opinionated, kind, outspoken, shy, competitive, insecure, confident…)
Individual responses will vary.

Optional Discussion Question
a) Was it difficult to include negative adjectives in your description of yourself?

9. List any personal habits that you find yourself involved in doing. It may help to review your personality traits if you are having a difficult time. The habits can be good or bad. (Smoking, speaking without thinking, thinking of others before yourself….)
Individual responses will vary.

10. Review the list, and separate them into the categories of <u>negative traits</u> and <u>positive</u> traits.
Individual responses will vary.

DAY THREE
Questions #11- #12 were individual assignments that do not need to be discussed.

13. Today, you are going to pray and ask God to reveal the areas in your life where you need to P.A.U.S.E (Pray and Use Self-Evaluation) and allow God to do a Spiritual alignment. You can refer to the prayer that I modeled in day two.

After you spend some time in prayer, outline one or more of the areas that God brought to your attention.

Individual responses will vary.

1) Identify the Habit/Behavior
2) Does it help me to grow in my spiritual life?
3) Does it build me up as a person?
4) Does it line up with biblical principles?
5) Does the habit/behavior cause negative consequences in your family tree?
6) Identify the lesson that was learned

DAY FOUR

Questions #14- #15 were individual assignments that do not need to be discussed.

16. As God has revealed another layer that He is refining, you need to submit to the process and take these necessary steps as well. Only then will you be able to conquer those obstacles that are holding you back in your weight loss goals.

Steps to the Healing Process

- **Step 1**: *Recognize* what has been holding you back from being prosperous in all areas of your life. Get out of denial so that you will be able to move forward toward victory.

  In all your ways acknowledge Him and He will direct your paths. **Proverbs 3:6**

- **Step 2**: *Release* yourself from guilt and be honest with yourself and with God. Tell Him that you are sorry. He loves you so much and He wants the best for you. He wants you to live an awesome life and let the light that He has given you to be present in all that you do. You were not created to do it on our own, so He is your personal shepherd to guide you.

If we confess our sins, he is faithful and just to forgive us our sins and to cleanse us from all unrighteousness. **I John 1:9**

- **Step 3**: *Repent* and turn away from any actions that hurt your Father. You can write a personal prayer to God to let Him know how much you love Him.

For the kind of sorrow God wants us to experience leads us away from sin and results in salvation. There's no regret for that kind of sorrow. But worldly sorrow, which lacks repentance, results in spiritual death. **2 Corinthians 7:10**

- **Step 4**: *Replace* any negativity with Scriptures and prayer to combat the attacks of the enemy.

Finally, brothers and sisters, whatever is true, whatever is noble, whatever is right, whatever is pure, whatever is lovely, whatever is admirable — if anything is excellent or praiseworthy — think about such things. **Philippians 4:8**

- **Step 5**: *Receive* God's unconditional love for you. He will always be there with His arms open wide to forgive you of any wrongdoings.

See how very much our Father loves us, for he

calls us his children, and that is what we are! But the people who belong to this world don't recognize that we are God's children because they don't know him. **I John 3:1**

17. Refer to the list of negative traits and habits that you developed in day three. Create a list of Bible verses that you can meditate on when the temptation to repeat negative behaviors confronts you.
Have participants share verses. Encourage group members to add the shared scriptures to their list.

DAY FIVE
Questions #18- #19 were individual assignments that do not need to be discussed.

20. Write a letter to God in the form of a prayer. Refer to the lesson you learned in day three from this week?
Individual responses will vary.

Optional Discussion Question
a) Did God reveal anything to you during your fasting experience?

Reflections for the Journey Ahead
- If time permits, read over the questions and allow participants time to answer complete the assignment and share responses. Otherwise, they may complete it on their

own time.

- Remind students to pre-plan their meals for the upcoming week
- End in prayer and remind participants to stay in contact with their partners throughout the week.

8

VICTORY IS ON THE HORIZON

- **Open in Prayer**
- **Ice Breaker Activity** – For this activity, you need to make sure to have a large bowl or a small bucket filled with water. Give each participant a sheet of paper and a pen. Have each person write down every negative or hurtful word or comment that has ever been said to them or about them. Tell participants that they can refer back to the previous weekly assignments to help them to remember. You may want to have some calm music playing softly in the background to stimulate the reflection process. After participants are finished, they may share if they so desire and have them fold the paper multiple times and place it in the bowl of water. This is symbolic of burying the past hurts and moving forward in the life of abundance that God desires for his children. Please allow quiet time for prayer and reflection before asking the following questions:
  1) How did you feel about this activity?
  2) What past hurts if any are you still holding on to?

Scripture Support:

    a. For I am about to do something new. See, I have already begun! Do you not see it? I will make a pathway through the wilderness. I will create rivers in the dry wasteland. **Isaiah 43:19**

- **Motivational Memory Verse**

Love is patient and kind. Love is not jealous or boastful or proud or rude. It does not demand its own way. It is not irritable, and it keeps no record of being wronged. It does not rejoice about injustice but rejoices whenever the truth wins out. I Corinthians 13:4-6

- **Weekly Overview**- Read aloud.
- **Weight Management Challenge**
  1) Have you increased your water consumption?
  2) How did the increase in water affect your eating habits this week?
- **Exercise Prompt**
  1) What exercise plan did you follow this week?
  2) Did you find a mentor?
     Encourage participants to continue to connect with their accountability partner with their exercising and weight management goals.
- **Chapter Reading** – Chapter 11

DAY ONE

Questions #1- #3 were individual assignments that do not need to be discussed.

- How many people pre-planned their meals for the week?
- What unhealthy foods did you eat last week that were not listed on your planner?
- What is your plan to stay on track this week?

4. What stands out in the reading that you can apply to your own life?
Individual responses will vary.

DAY TWO

Questions #5- #6 were individual assignments that do not need to be discussed.

7. Write about a negative experience you have encountered when people in your personal life have made assumptions about you or made you feel uncomfortable because you are overweight.
Individual responses will vary.

Optional Discussion Question
a) Was it difficult to recollect the memory or was it fresh in your mind?

8. How did that make you feel? Embarrassed? Self-Conscious? Angry? Etc...
Individual responses will vary.

a) Does that experience/assumption still impact you today? If so, how does it impact you.

9. Have you forgiven that person? If you have not extended forgiveness, write your thoughts. If you have forgiven them, write your thoughts on what you will do if it happens again.
Individual responses will vary. This may be difficult for participants to share.

10. If you lack forgiveness for someone, what does Matthew 5:24 say about forgiveness?
Leave your gift there in front of the altar. First go and be reconciled to them; then come and offer your gift.
Matthew 5:24

Prayer of Forgiveness

Dear Jesus,

There are people that have hurt me and words cannot fully describe how much pain they have caused. I know that you understand my pain because you were also hurt by people that said that they loved you. You said in your Holy Scriptures that in order for you to forgive me, that I must forgive others (Matthew 6:15). Forgiving them for their wrongdoings is not easy for me, but I know that I can do it with your help. Please forgive me, heal my heart and teach me how to forgive them as you have forgiven me.

Amen

DAY THREE

Questions #11- #12 were individual assignments that do not need to be discussed.

13. Another area that the devil tries to manipulate and control people is in the area of condemnation. Forgiveness does not only apply to others, but also to oneself. Holding on to guilt is a sign of unforgiveness. I struggled with guilt for secretly binging and overeating. As a result, I did not fully love and accept myself when I got on the scale. Are there areas in your life where you struggle with guilt? Does my story of a guilty conscious sound familiar?

Individual responses will vary. This may be difficult for participants to share.

<u>Optional Discussion Question</u>

a) When you get on the scale, what emotions do you experience?

14. What does Romans 8:1 say about us condemning ourselves?

So now there is no condemnation for those who belong to Christ Jesus. **Romans 8:1**

15. According to Revelations 12:10, who is our accuser? *Satan*

If God be truth as it is written in Romans 3:4, then we need to rid ourselves of guilt and walk in forgiveness in every area of our life. We cannot let the enemy have any control in this area of our life; you do not want to walk in a life filled with guilt, shame, rejection, hatred and other tactics the enemy of your soul may use to gain leverage in your thoughts and actions. Allow the words of the following prayer to penetrate your heart and heal you from the guilt of your past.

Prayer for Self-Forgiveness

Dear Heavenly Father,

You do not want me to live my life condemning myself, but to walk in freedom through your Holy Spirit. I repent for holding on to negative emotions and labels and not embracing the women/man you have called me to be. I now receive your love and will not align myself with Satan's accusations against what you have created as wonderful and beautiful according to your Holy words that say, "I will praise You, for I am fearfully and wonderfully made; Marvelous are Your works, And that my soul knows very well" (Psalms 139:14).

Amen

DAY FOUR

Questions #16- #17 were individual assignments that do not need to be discussed.

18. God has gifted each of us with unique talents and abilities. What talents and gifts has God given to you?

Individual responses will vary.

19. We are instructed as Christians to use whatever gifts we have received to serve others, as faithful stewards of God's grace (I Peter 4:10). When serving in ministry, you want to use your talents from a place of healing and not from a place of hurt. God wants to use those healings from the hurts and struggles to become a blessing for the body of Christ. What ideas or ministries is God planting in your heart?

Individual responses will vary.

Optional Discussion Question

a) How can you use your experiences to help others?

DAY FIVE

Questions #20- #21 were individual assignments that do not need to be discussed.

22. In Chapter 7, I shared a conversation that I had with God regarding writing a book about my personal weight struggles. Just as I felt that pull to do something to bless others, you should have that longing as well. Is there anything blocking you from pursuing those desires? What is it?

Individual responses will vary.

a) What steps do you need to take in order to pursue your mission?

23. Are any of them related to insecurities? Fears? Shortcomings? What have you learned so far in regards to those concerns?
Individual responses will vary.

Reflections for the Journey Ahead
- If time permits, read over the questions and allow participants time to answer complete the assignment and share responses. Otherwise, they may complete it on their own time.
- Remind students to pre-plan their meals for the upcoming week
- End in prayer and remind participants to stay in contact with their partners throughout the week.

ENCOURAGEMENT FOR THE JOURNEY AHEAD

Have participants take turns reading the P.R.O.U.D Moments acronym below and offer comments on how they can apply it to their daily life. Encourage participants to begin *A Journal for Your Weight Loss Journey: Guided Reflections and Words of Encouragement* as a way to stay focused on their commitment to getting fit. Accountability partners should stay in frequent contact with one another and consider continuing to meet as a group frequently to encourage each other and to reconnect.

PAUSE ON FITNESS P.R.O.U.D MOMENTS

P-Pause & Pray
Acknowledge God in everything by stopping to pray. This includes accepting that overeating leads to undesirable outcomes. Divine help can be utilized to get past overindulgences and weak moments. God will intervene if you allow him; you do not have to worry about fighting this temptation alone.

R- Recognize & Reflect
This is a moment to reflect on God's goodness and recognize who you are in Christ. You are secure,

you are accepted, you are loved, you are a friend of God, you are free from condemnation and you are a child of God! Hold your head up high and walk in the confidence that God will complete the work that He started.

O-Open & Obey

Be open to what God wants to reveal to you. He will give you the strategy to overcome any temptations that you encounter. You need to be still, listen to His voice and obey Him. He may put a song in your heart, bring a Scripture to your remembrance or even tell you to do something out of the ordinary. Whatever God says to you, trust that He will always provide an escape if you first acknowledge Him.

U- Utilize & Understand

Utilize the tools that are around you. Seek out a mentor, accountability partner and other role models that can assist you. Continue to use the lessons in this book and research other authors that you can connect with. Most importantly, understand that this journey is a process and that it is all right to ask for help.

D-Delight & Deny

Delight yourself in the things of God. Ask God to refresh you with His presence, so that you do not seek food or other indulgences to fill a void. Spend time in the Word of God and allow the Scriptures to become life to your body. God's presence is life; make a commitment to die to your old ways and bad habits in order to take on the mind of Christ each day. Sometimes that requires you to deny yourself in order to gain the prize ahead!

OTHER BOOKS BY THE AUTHOR

Empowering Youth with Purpose
ISBN 1-46356-076-1
An incredible book to help assist in the
incredible calling to mentor and to educate youth
in a secular environment.

The Devil Wants Me Fat: Lessons to Inspire,
Empower and Overcome
ISBN 978-0692646113
Stephanie shares an autobiographical account
of her personal struggles and victories with weight
loss and takes readers on her personal journey to
have a definitive answer to whether or not it is a
sin to be fat.

A Journal for Your Weight Loss Journey
ISBN 978-0692273432
A self-reflective journal that uses Bible
scriptures, weight loss stories, pictures, poems,
words of encouragement, quotes and writing
prompts to help people to stay focused on their
fitness goals.

All books are available online at
www.Pause66.com